LIVING
MY
TRUTH

LIVING MY TRUTH

LEADING BEYOND CONTRADICTIONS, COMPROMISE AND CORPORATIONS

ALAN K. NEVEL

Verity Publishing
Cleveland

VERITY PUBLISHING

VERITAS ETHICAS
INTEGRITAS

ISBN: 978-1-7371443-7-3

Published by:
Verity Publishing, LLC
Cleveland, Ohio, USA

First Edition: February 2025
This book is a work of nonfiction based on the author's personal experiences. The author and publisher are not responsible for any outcomes resulting from the use of the information in this book. For inquiries, please contact:
anevel@intethiq.com | www.intethiq.com

About the Author

Alan K. Nevel is the CEO and Managing Partner of INTETHIQ, a management consultancy and professional services firm dedicated to helping businesses navigate cultural, leadership, talent, and digital transformations.

With over 30 years of leadership experience, Alan has a proven track record of fostering equitable workplaces, driving inclusive systems, and delivering impactful programs at global Fortune 500 companies.

Before launching INTETHIQ in 2023, Alan served as Senior Vice President, Chief Equity and Community Impact Officer at The MetroHealth System in Cleveland, Ohio, where he led diversity, equity, and inclusion initiatives and worked to dismantle healthcare disparities.

His previous roles include VP, Global Diversity and Inclusion at Thermo Fisher Scientific and leadership positions at both L Brands and Victoria's Secret.

Alan began his career in R&D and manufacturing at Sherwin-Williams before transitioning to consulting at Accenture.

Alan holds a B.A. from Cleveland State University and an MBA from Case Western Reserve University, where he also teaches as an Adjunct Professor. Alan actively supports education and community development through various local and national board director roles and scholarships.

Acknowledgments

There are so many people who have come in and out, and even back again, throughout my life. Those of you who know me know what you've meant to me. And every single one of you has played a role in the writing of this book.

To "Blackliffe," I thank you. To Wickliffe, I thank you.

To Lee-Seville, I thank you. To The Bond, I thank you.

To the InTENtional Men of Faith, I thank you.

To Brother Gene, I thank you.

To all of my Friends, I thank you.

To my ENTIRE FAMILY, I thank you.

And last but not least, thanks be to God for always being there when I didn't realize it, and most certainly didn't deserve it!

Foreword

Many years ago, I read a statement in one of Iyanla Vanzant's books, "People come into our lives for a reason, a season or a lifetime." But when I think about Alan K. Nevel, I realize that our lives have intersected for different reasons in different seasons throughout our lifetimes. He is much more than my brother from another mother. Alan is truly my brother in Christ.

We "officially" met in the late 1990s or early 2000s, when we both served on the Board of Directors for Karamu House Theater, the oldest African American producing theater in the country. After that season came to an end, our paths crossed again at the Diversity Center of Northeast Ohio's Humanitarian Dinner in 2018. I believe the reason for that brief reconnection was simply to set the stage for what was to come.

As the COVID pandemic unfolded alongside the unrest fueled by the senseless killings of George Floyd, Ahmaud Arbery, Brianna Taylor, and so many others, our paths crossed yet again through our work in the DEI space.

In 2024, Alan and I were discussing the changes that had occurred in his life that ultimately led to him starting his company, INTETHIQ. The more we talked about what, if any, opportunities might exist for us to work together through INTETHIQ, something else came to light.

Alan mentioned he was working on this book, and everything clicked into place. God gave me clarity that this was the reason our paths had been crossing for more than two decades. When I told Alan this, he sent me a copy of his manuscript, and I was captivated by the stories he shared about his life.

I was shocked to find out just how many times our paths must have crossed without our even knowing it, how much our life stories have in common.

My hope is that all those who read this book will find similar points of connection within Alan's story.

That you will find inspiration and encouragement to continue moving forward on your journey.

That you will see pain and heartache can actually become the fuel for finding your passion and purpose in life, just as Alan did.

The life lessons that led Alan to write this book help us see there is a leader inside each of us, whether in our homes, on our jobs, or within our communities.

Written from a place of honesty, authenticity, and transparency, *"Living MY Truth: Leading Beyond Contradictions, Compromise and Corporations"* is sure to spark those AHA Moments that will shine a light on your path to becoming the leader you were destined to be.

May it give you the confidence to live your truth as you use your gifts in service to others.

Rev. Heidi L. Barham

Contents

Prologue

On October 9, 2023, I resigned from a high- powered, $500,000-a-year+ job at The MetroHealth System in Cleveland, Ohio, so I could live a better life.

I knew what I wanted: a purposeful union of personal and professional goals, activities, and aspirations that would draw on my fifty-nine years of experience – failures as well as successes – in order to elevate others around me.

That included being told at the age of three that I was the man of the house. Growing up in a supportive, nurturing, predominately Black and Italian neighborhood in a small town and dreaming of professional football stardom. Navigating a fraught relationship with my brilliant but haunted mother who was entering the last months of her life.

Flunking out of two colleges – the first one when I was on scholarship. Getting a third chance for redemption at Cleveland State University. Enjoying successful careers in research and development, manufacturing, human resources, and diversity, equity, and inclusion.

Failing at one marriage and later thriving with my childhood sweetheart.

I knew I had the skills and qualities to make a difference, but often I applied them in opposite directions. My leadership had both inspired a manufacturing team to greater productivity and established an off-campus house where the party never stopped. My persuasiveness had brought me both high-level corporate jobs and a high number of cannabis-smoking colleagues and customers.

My work ethic had both earned me promotions and masked the dark side of my double life. The inner struggle was exhausting. I wanted to transcend the contradictions. I wanted to express leadership integrity, ethics, authenticity, transparency, and vulnerability. No more hiding. I was growing spiritually, confident of a call to something greater, but I was surrounded by conflicting values at work.

The initiatives I led were considered successful, but I was dissatisfied with their lack of long-lasting impact to transform our community. I wanted to make a real difference in the lives of others.

I wanted to make a real difference in my own life. So, I quit.

The leap of faith liberated me to be fully who I am and to fulfill my Eternal Father's purpose. This required not only trust but also complete surrender.

All the pieces came together when I launched INTETHIQ, a business expression of myself in union with my personal vision, values, and principles.

Chances are, my story touches your story – maybe as echo, maybe as inspiration, maybe as cautionary tale.

I am not alone in this world that so often seeks profit over people, self-interest over solidarity, masks over authenticity.

Neither are you.

My Shoebox

Many years ago, I participated in a teambuilding exercise designed to give each person a chance to share a glimpse into their world. This exercise started with an empty shoebox to hold a collection of the person's random artifacts that most resonated with them and represented who they uniquely were. I still have mine. This book lets you look inside my world – the good, the bad, and the ugly – as life keeps adding more mementos every day.

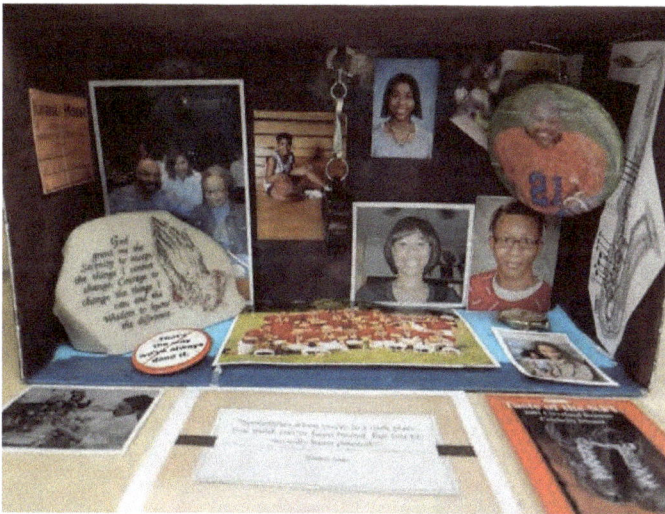

Three-Year-Old Man of the House

When I was three years old, my mother told me: "You're the man of the house." I believed her. That set the course for my life, as those enduring words have so largely defined me to this day.

Me

I grew up in two very different worlds. On the weekends, I lived in the eastern Cleveland suburb of Wickliffe with my dog Pixie and my Mom Evelyn. She had split from my father in 1965, when I was eighteen months old, after nine years of marriage. During the work week, I lived with my maternal grandparents on the southeast side of Cleveland, Ohio in the Lee-Seville neighborhood.

Momma and Daddy's House

"Big Momma and Daddy" had moved from Vicksburg, Mississippi to Cleveland during the Great Migration of Black people from the South seeking better jobs and better lives in the North. My Mom, her parents, and four siblings arrived in Cleveland in 1943.

Daddy, My Mom and Her Siblings

My neighborhoods in Wickliffe and Cleveland could not have been any more different from one another.

Wickliffe was a predominately white, working class community with its racial diversity being isolated to a collection of seven streets that we affectionately referred to as "Blackliffe".

The Lee-Seville neighborhood where my grandparents lived in Cleveland was all black. While these communities at first glance "looked" vastly different, the experiences and early life lessons that I had, highlighted our shared humanity.

Our family also owned a farm about forty miles east of Cleveland, in a small rural community called Windsor, where my cousins and I would chase chickens and play outside until sundown. Most of our weekends involved family cookouts on the grill, with us kids running around playing on the grounds and the adults playing checkers or bid whist while drinking, laughing, and arguing.

It was just me and my Mom growing up. I recall having seen my father only twice as a child – on my fifth birthday in 1969 and then three years later when I got home from Harrisburg, Pennsylvania, after I was in a terrible accident. I was nineteen before I saw him again, at a birthday party for his mother, Beatrice O. Nevel.

Because my parents were married for nine years before I was born, I grew up assuming that my birth contributed to their separation and eventual divorce.

My Dad and Mom

I struggled for years wondering why my father never reached out to me – he and his family lived in the suburb of Cleveland Heights, which was less than a half-hour away from me in Wickliffe. I was always told that he abandoned US. I discovered in my late forties that there was another side to this story.

There are always two sides of every story, with the truth residing somewhere in between. My Mom had actively kept him away while consistently telling me he didn't want anything to do with US.

While my father was nowhere near perfect, and some of the stories that Mom shared about him were true, that should not have denied ME the opportunity to build a relationship.

I believe that a child needs both parents in their lives, and parenting is a shared responsibility irrespective of their relationship with each other. I often longed for an adult male figure to talk to, yet I was often left to wing it. Simply put, my life is evidence that no one is the perfect spouse or parent.

We all must do the best we can with what knowledge we have and hope to keep our mistakes to a minimum.

A few years before my father died in 2017, I discovered he had never stopped carrying the same baby picture of me in his wallet that Mom carried in hers, in addition to saving numerous press clippings of my academic and athletic achievements.

The Picture in the Wallet

That was when I realized that my father had actually always loved me.

He never made any disparaging remarks about my Mom or their years together, and the few times they met in person, he always complimented her on raising a good son.

Every time I left him after a visit, he hugged me, shed a few tears, and said, "I'm sorry." Too many of us miss the chance to admit our frailties, or say "I'm sorry," and have the chance to restore our relationships before death. Sometimes this can lead to missed opportunities and regrets.

I am forever grateful for the loving adult relationship that I had with my father. I now have a sense of closure.

Me and My Dad

Mom

Mom was the first Black chemist at Lubrizol Corporation's Wickliffe headquarters. That was a rare achievement for a woman of color in the 1960s and 1970s, and the company always included her lighter- skinned, "exotic" picture in its black-and-white annual reports. Unfortunately, she was only paid a lab technician's salary until two years before she retired. The gender pay inequity was even more pronounced in those days. This type of indignity is still ongoing across many industries

Mom (1969)

Mom (1980)

When I was in my fifties, I learned that our seven street neighborhood in Wickliffe was called "Little Africa" by outsiders for its predominantly Black population; most who weren't African American were of Italian descent.

As children, we shared a love of food. My white friends ate collard and mustard greens, blackeyed peas and crackling corn bread with me, and I ate pasta, sunday gravy, and cannolis with them. We also shared an identity as Wickliffe Blue Devils and that was something that transcended race or ethnicity.

I was never called the "n-word" by my white classmates, and my teammates often stood up to the racist vitriol from visiting white athletic rivals. We were just a bunch of kids growing up together and enjoying our shared humanity.

Back then, Wickliffe was one of those places where you didn't have to lock your doors at night. I also remember that you could get a spanking from a friend's parents when you misbehaved at their house and then get another when you got home.

Our House

One the things that to this day I believe I was born with is a strong work ethic. My first job, at age three, involved taking my grandfather's Red Wing boots off when he came home from his second job, setting them on the back stoop, and opening a can of Carling's Black Label beer for him.

Alcohol and its abuse have impacted me from the beginning. Daddy always expected me to take the last swig from his can before I brought him the next one. When I was four, I passed out drunk because I was running beer from the cooler to a room full of partying adults who all gave me their last swigs.

As compensation for my weekly job, Daddy paid me a case quarter every Friday, which I took to Mr. Powell's corner store to buy a sack filled with twenty-five pieces of penny candy. This connection between work and reward instilled both a work ethic and a precocious bent to entrepreneurship.

My sole remaining treasure from my grandfather is the gold watch he received for working twenty-five years as a machinist at the General Motors Fisher Body Division plant. While it has become mostly a collection of broken pieces and parts, I cherish it to this day.

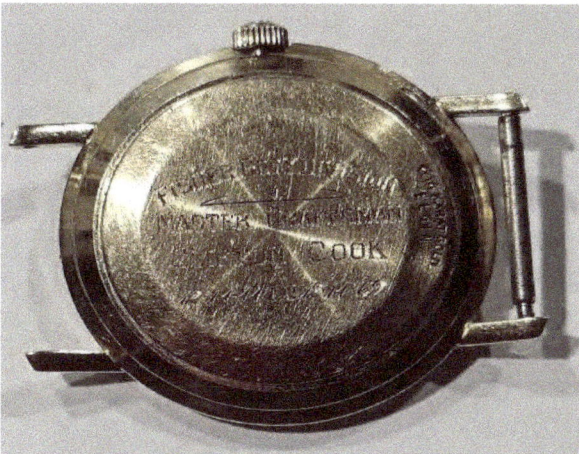

Daddy's Watch

In addition to his GM job, Daddy worked at the Cloverleaf Drive-In Theater in nearby Garfield Heights. He took my oldest cousin, Anthony, and me with him to help repair the speakers that hooked over customers' car windows and to clean the drive-in theater grounds and concession stand area. Daddy paid us in popcorn and orange-flavored syrup, the basis of carbonated orange drink. Anthony, who was five years older, was the son of my Aunt BeBe and often stayed with me at our grandparents' house. I grew up wanting to be just like him – scholar, football player, track star, everything.

Anthony and Me

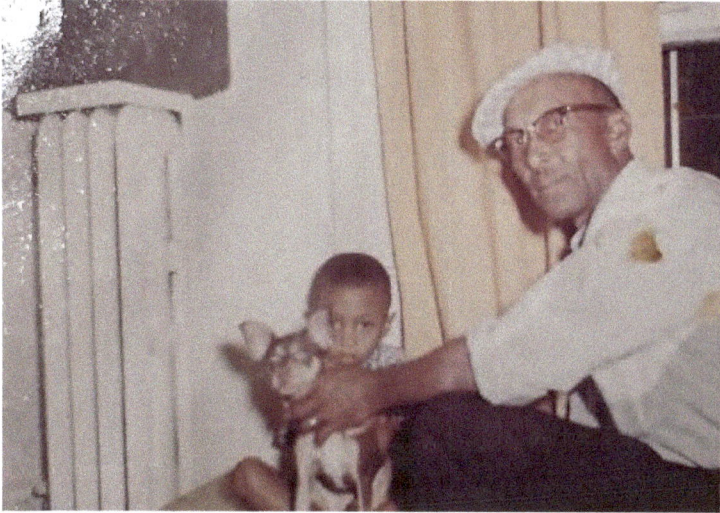

Anthony, Daddy and My Dog, Pixie

Anthony at Antioch College

My Mom always credited Daddy with holding our extended family together. When he unexpectedly died of a heart attack in his sleep in June 1970, when I was six years old, our lives suddenly changed.

The weekly weekend gatherings on Chateau Avenue dwindled to mostly holidays.

Whenever we were together, a tension hung in the air, like something wasn't being said that should.

After Daddy passed, my Mom started drinking more. I had convinced her to quit smoking (mostly by getting her to watch anti-smoking commercials during Saturday morning cartoons), but she took it up again for about six months before she finally quit for good.

As I look back so many years after my grandfather died, I realize a piece of my Mom died with him then.

Daddy and My Mom

Mom and her siblings each had a unique relationship with Big Momma – Aunt HErma (pronounced "Her – Ma") was close to her while Mom was much more distant because as a child she had to care for her younger siblings when Big Momma was on one of her many trips to visit with family.

Uncle Cliff, who like Mom was held back two grades when they emigrated to Cleveland, was a very violent and angry man; in fact, Mom never let me be alone with him. I recall him physically fighting with his very own father and even my Mom, once landing her in the hospital!

She always said Uncle Cliff was the most sweet and gentle child you could have imagined before they moved North, and she blamed the change in his demeanor on his being held back in school as well as his relentless need to prove his toughness despite his short stature as soon as they reached Cleveland.

I guess he decided at some point to become the bully instead of the bullied.

"No individual is perfect. No family is perfect. No community is perfect. We all have issues, so show grace to yourself and to those who are around you."

Aunt HErma & Big Momma

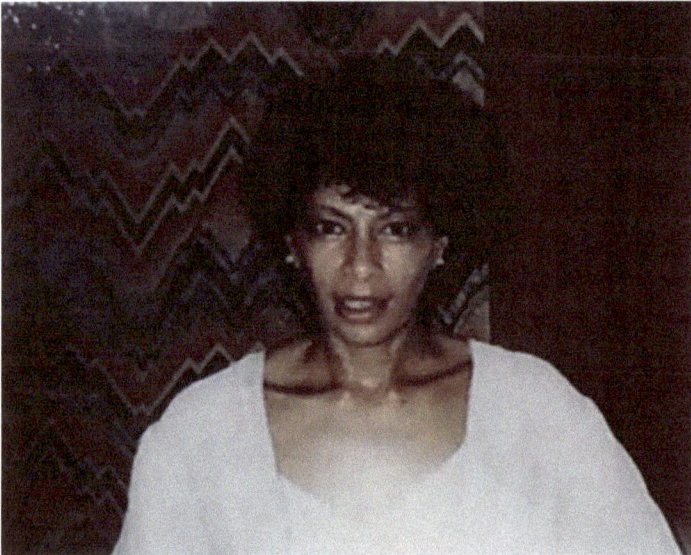

Aunt BeBe

A Hustler's Mentality

With Daddy's example, I developed a hustler's mentality at an early age. When I was nine, I delivered the Cleveland *Call and Post*, a Black newspaper; when I was thirteen, I fried fish and chips at Arthur Treacher's Restaurant, where grease would pop up and burn my hands and arms. During high school, I moved on to work at Ponderosa Steak House.

Back then, I tried hard to follow my Mom's advice about money: save a third of each paycheck, pay bills with a third, and spend a third, or as she put it: "pay the bank, pay your bills, pay yourself."

I also learned pretty early how to build a team, motivate, and inspire others, like Tom Sawyer's knack for recruiting people to help with work. Our back yard was the neighborhood sports field when we were too young to walk to the park by ourselves. My friends teased me because I sang the theme from the Saturday morning NFL Game of the Week replay while we played football.

When I had to cut the grass, I convinced my friends that we could start playing sooner if we worked together.

We took turns cutting a few rows, and if the grass was tall, somebody would rake the clippings. We all pushed as fast as we could.

Perhaps it didn't really save much time, but we all felt we had helped get the game going.

"Individually, we can accomplish much, but together, we can achieve what none of us could alone."

Dead or Alive?

On the way back from a church field trip to Philadelphia in April 1972, when I was in second grade, we were in a terrible bus accident that killed four passengers.

My Mom broke four vertebrae in her back, Big Momma broke her hip and shoulder, Aunt BeBe broke her wrist, and my cousin Anthony and I suffered an assortment of bumps, scrapes, and bruises. Remarkably, my two-and-a- half-year-old cousin Dawn was pulled from the wreckage without even a scratch.

However, our close friend Simone, who grew up with us like a cousin, was ejected from the bus onto the Pennsylvania Turnpike and killed. One other child died, a boy who was mistaken for me at first – the Cleveland Press reported I died in the crash, while the Cleveland Plain Dealer said I survived.

When I returned to Wickliffe and Lincoln Elementary School several weeks later, some of my classmates were astonished to see me.

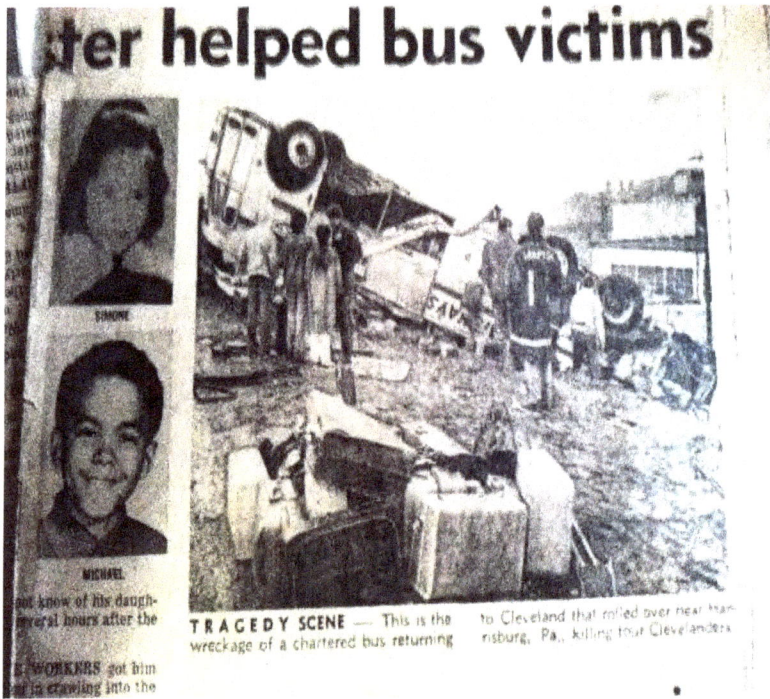

Cleveland Plain Dealer Article, April 1972

The accident even made national news, including the New York Times on April 17, 1972.

4 Dead, 43 Hurt in Pennsylvania Turnpike Bus Crash

Rescue workers carry victim away from overturned bus on turnpike near Harrisburg

HARRISBURG, Pa., April 16 (AP)—Four persons were killed and 43 injured today when a chartered bus crashed through a guardrail on the rain-slick Pennsylvania Turnpike near here and overturned.

The bus landed on its roof, halfway down a slight hill, pinning the passengers inside. Firemen broke through the windows to take out the dead and injured.

A turnpike police spokesman said the Continental Trailways bus was chartered by the Present Day Baptist Church in Cleveland.

The church group of 46 persons was returning home to Cleveland after a weekend of sightseeing in Philadelphia, according to United Press International.

The driver, Joseph McPengano, 26, of Pittsburgh, said

that all he remembered before the crash was that "two cars were blocking the middle of the road." He said he applied the brakes and the bus began to skid.

There were 48 persons on the bus at the time of the accident—46 passengers, a tour director and the driver.

The accident occurred one-quarter mile west of the Harrisburg-East Interchange.

The New York Times
Published: April 17, 1972
Copyright © The New York Times

"Everything that people think or say about you may not always be true."

Football

The game of football was my first love for most of my childhood.

When I was four, Mom took me on the rapid-transit bus to Cleveland Municipal Stadium to sit in the bleachers and watch my very first Browns game – the AFL Championship against the Baltimore Colts.

We enjoyed a broad sense of family in those days – everyone in our section shared whatever they brought to the game.

We often stopped by Pudgie's Famous Chicken on Euclid Avenue and picked up a bucket of fried chicken to contribute.

My love for the game involved both watching it and playing it – in more than one way.

Mom gave me a Tudor Games electric football set in 1970, with the Cleveland Browns and the New York Jets, who played the first-ever Monday Night Football game.

I collected every NFL team, in both their home and away uniforms, before the Houston Oilers became the Tennessee Titans, the Colts moved to Indianapolis, and the Cardinals moved to St. Louis, then Los Angeles, then Arizona.

Sometimes, we sprinkled salt on the metal "football field" to simulate   snow   on   the   ground.

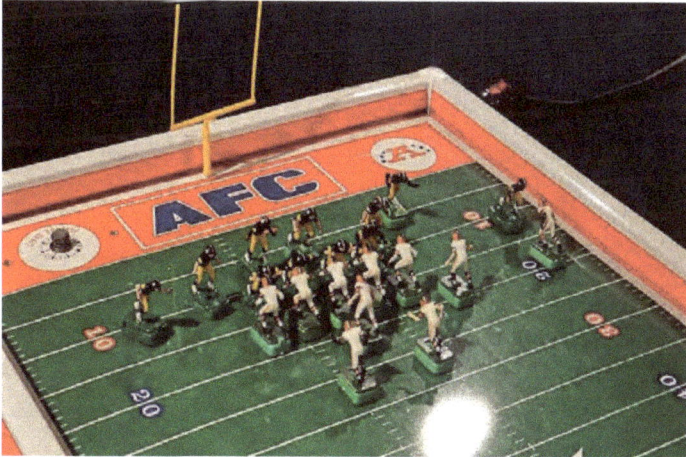

For as long as I can remember, I wanted to play quarterback – the leader of the team. In our neighborhood pick-up games, I was always the quarterback and even won our local area NFL Punt, Pass, and Kick competition at age nine.

In those days, most people thought players who looked like me could never play a "cerebral" position like quarterback. Maybe at the collegiate level, but certainly not professionally.

There were only two Black quarterbacks in the National Football League at that time, both backups – James "Shack" Harris of the Los Angeles Rams and "Jefferson Street" Joe Gilliam of our bitter rival, the Pittsburgh Steelers.

Although I aspired to become an NFL quarterback, I played offensive guard at age eight for the Cincinnati Bengals lightweight division team my first year in the Wickliffe Midget Football League. After that season, and all through high school, I played running back except with one season as defensive back.

At five feet, six-and-a-half inches tall, I wasn't really built to play quarterback, even in junior high, but few things could keep me from competing to the best of my abilities and challenging the status quo.

My Mom supported my free-thinking and decision-making, often over Big Momma and other adult's objections.

During my senior year, Wickliffe played our arch-rival Lake Catholic for the unofficial "Lake County Championship" and was televised on WVIZ Channel 25. At the bottom of a pileup after one play, a Lake Catholic defender twisted my ankle so hard I had to be carried off the field.

A few days later, I learned a bone in my ankle was chipped. An individual on the sideline handed me a pill while they taped my ankle and shoe, and I went back in feeling no pain.

For the rest of the season, I spent most weekday practices in a training room taking hot/cold   treatments,
participated   in   the   Thursday walkthroughs with helmets and shorts, and played every game with "a little extra help" from those pills.

Sadly, we just missed out on the playoffs when we lost our last regular-season game to Solon High School - 3 to 0.

I also ran track in high school and was on the 4x100 meter relay team, which held the school record for over thirty-five years. Every now and then, one of us would end up calling the school to make sure none of our records had been broken.

1982 Wickliffe Night Relays Championship Trophy

We were all enormously proud to be Wickliffe Blue Devils. Our track and field coach Al Benz liked to brag, "Everyone in the stadium takes notice when the Blue Devils arrive."

While my graduating class in 1982 had more than three hundred eighty students, the school now graduates about one hundred students a year and has dropped athletically all the way down from Division II back then to Division V present day.

Always A Blue Devil

We athletes were close. In late 2023, I attended the funeral of Mr. Oliver Porter, the father of a dear friend and teammate who lived on my street when we were growing up.

Coach Benz was there, almost eighty years old, and still coaching. Two close friends and teammates came up from Texas for this reunion under sad circumstances. We laughed as we remembered that I was always the party organizer, a different kind of leadership skill that I ultimately grew further into.

The funeral service took place in the same church where my Mom taught 4th Grade Sunday School.

I spoke on behalf of myself and my best friend and teammate, Sid, who couldn't come up from Atlanta, Georgia. Sid and I were two of the few boys in our neighborhood without a man in the house, and revered Mr. Porter as being a great role model and strong black man.

All of us made our fair share of dumb mistakes and poor choices as adolescents, teens, and even young adults, but our close-knit neighborhood was rich with such men whose words and actions helped us to grow up and become productive citizens.

"You never know who's watching, so your life has the potential to become a shining example to others."

A Double Life

As great as it was, growing up in Wickliffe came with a dark side. Alcohol and drug abuse was prevalent in our community, not any different than what has plagued many urban and rural areas across our nation.

This four- square-mile town once hosted more than thirty establishments that sold or served alcohol. Four bars were within a hundred yards of my street along Euclid Avenue. The culture also introduced children to wine.

When I was barely a toddler, my babysitter from Italy asked my Mom to pick up a bottle of Chianti while grocery shopping, because she believed all babies should drink an ounce of wine each day for their health.

My Mom and many others made wine and home brew. We had Niagara and Catawba grapevines in our yard, as well as cherry, apple, peach, and pear trees, and the kids would stomp grapes in the wine press to extract the juice.

We adopted marijuana while we were young, imitating what we saw some of the older kids doing. Alcohol and drugs inevitably led to other unsavory activities, with the younger kids serving as lookouts to alert everyone when the parents were close by.

Throughout my growing up in Wickliffe, I succeeded in school despite the partying. I had no real study skills, but I could remember what my teachers said long enough to get the right answer on a test.

I was also a two-sport athlete, football and track, and played saxophone in both the concert and jazz bands.

I was elected class president my sophomore year, served on student council throughout high school, and was a member of the locally televised Academic Challenge team my junior and senior years.

Academic Challenge Team Junior Year (Fall 1990)

I took mostly advanced college-prep classes, where I was the only person of color in the room – only band and physical education included other Black students.

This deeply troubled me all throughout elementary, junior high, and high school. Why was I the only one in the room? Was there something wrong with me? Was I black enough, or was I "trying to be white"? Where did I fit in?

This struggle left me prone to engage in risky behaviors, to try and out-drink and out-smoke others, especially neighborhood kids, to prove that I was just like them.

Thus began a nearly fifteen-year cascade of self-inflicted wounds that tore at my mind, body, soul, and relationships with friends, family, and loved ones.

"Every coin has two sides
but nevertheless retains its value"

College – Strikes 1 & 2

I earned mostly A's and a few B's in high school, and won an academic scholarship to Miami University in Oxford, Ohio. It was Fall 1982, and I was part of a record Black cohort at the self-proclaimed "Harvard of the Midwest."

There were one hundred eight of us, with more than half assigned to the South Quad area of campus.

The first week I was there, I was shocked to look outside my classroom window and see the Ku Klux Klan holding a public march. They had come across the Indiana state line about a mile away, marched into town, and then turned around and marched right back out.

This was when I had to start figuring out how to navigate an environment where I clearly didn't belong.

Some of my fellow Black students figured it out, while others eventually left, either voluntarily or involuntarily.

1983

Mom wanted me to become a pediatrician, a dream she never gave up on. But now, absent of the self-discipline required to participate in sports in high school, I spent most of my time partying and ultimately got kicked out after three semesters.

While I could potentially return after sitting out for a semester, I instead went home, earned straight A's at a local community college (no more of a challenge for myself than high school was), and got admitted in Fall 1984 to the University of Akron, in nearby Akron, Ohio.

By then, my entrepreneurial activities included selling weed and anything else you might want. My *modus operandi* was to sell you some weed, smoke it with you until it was gone, then sell you some more.

A few friends and I rented a house off-campus that eventually became known as the party headquarters, where we often spent hours listening to P-Funk along with "Jazz and J's."

Every day was spent mostly drinking malt liquor or cheap wine, smoking bud, and hanging out. As soon as I woke up to go to my work-study job in the dining hall, I smoked a joint or two. After I got off work, I smoked some more.

There were times when I was so messed up from the night before, that the little old ladies who worked in the dining hall would help me clock in for my shift and then sneak me into a back room to sleep it off.

While I was on campus every day, usually dressed in suits and ties and carrying a briefcase, I wasn't going to class.

I knew it was wrong. My Mom had taught me better. I was deliberately self-destructive, uncertain since grade school whether I was Black enough, and often feeling uncomfortable in my own skin.

I didn't love myself. I always felt I had to be in "proving mode." I never felt like I had done enough to truly belong.

I was a scholar for those who liked scholars, an athlete for those who liked athletes, a cool cat for those who liked cool, but I still didn't know who I really was, let alone who I wanted to be.

I got kicked out of the University of Akron in Spring 1986. I was eighteen credit hours short of a chemistry degree, but my GPA in that last semester was 0.79 out of a possible 4.00. I honestly didn't even know you could get below a 1.00 GPA, but somehow, I did.

So, I finally had to level with my Mom, not only about the University of Akron, but also about Miami University and the double life I had lived all those years.

To survive, I knew I needed to escape that environment, that life, and also some of the people who had befriended me.

"Many of us have negative experiences as children and even as young adults, but it is up to us to choose how we want to define ourselves moving forward."

The First Breakthrough

Knowing that I needed to clear my mind, body, and soul, Mom helped me get into a twenty-eight day residential program at a drug and alcohol treatment facility. This facility was located about an hour east of Cleveland.

While I was there, I began to grapple with some of my issues. No one knew I was there, except for my Mom, my girlfriend, and two close friends. I had just turned twenty-two years old.

At the treatment center, I saw people in their thirties, forties, and older who had lost families, jobs, everything because of substance abuse and its associated behaviors. Some of them had even done time. Getting kicked out of school twice seemed minor, because by the grace of God, I had never even been arrested.

After four days of detox and a battery of tests, they concluded that I was not chemically dependent on alcohol or drugs – even though I had tried cocaine on multiple occasions. I was addicted to the lifestyle and the high of living on the edge.

My physical activity, first in organized sports, then regular weightlifting and playing pickup basketball games, had somehow protected me.

There were people my age and even younger in the program who had severe cirrhosis of the liver from drinking, sniffing glue, and vaping aerosol cans of paint.

But by the grace of God, my body was still healthy.

The college failures replaced my cockiness with humility and taught me to begin slowly learning to forgive myself.

Now, I often share this story to help others. I have given talks to kids who come from meager circumstances, from those who spent their lives in foster care, not knowing if they would ever have a chance to go to college, to those driven to choose between furthering their education and dropping out of high school to work to provide for their younger siblings.

The past, no matter how dark, does not have to define us. WE get to decide how it fits into a story of service and success in the future.

While I was in the treatment center, my girlfriend Karen visited every weekend. She gathered up my belongings from various locations, and paid off my bills, including a Firestone credit card, all while working full-time and going to school part-time.

When I completed the program, we moved in together and I started looking for a job. Fortunately, I had participated in INROADS, a high school development program for talented minority students in business and science. For two summers, I worked as an intern at Britsh Petroleum's technical research center, located in nearby Warrensville Heights. The following summer, I worked at Lubrizol Corporation in Wickliffe.

Due to those internships, I had developed a pretty significant amount of chemical laboratory research and development experience.

I was fortunate to land a job with The Sherwin Williams Company creating all sorts of chemical formulations, from aerosol spray paints, to oils and lubricants, to insecticides, and even furniture polishes.

I was paid as an entry-level chemist and was assured the company would pay me to finish the roughly eighteen credit hours left to finish my bachelor's degree.

I felt plenty of awkward, isolated moments in the beginning, as the "only one" in the laboratory. There was minimal racial or ethnic diversity in the front offices. Other than a few Administrative Assistants, an HR Representative, and the Production Manager, everyone else who was black or brown worked in the factory.

Like many of my counterparts, colleagues and contemporaries, I often felt the pressure of having to represent my entire race. Simply put, I had to be twice as good in order to even be counted as close to equal.

Working in the Lab at Sherwin Williams

Whenever I had to go into the plant to pick up solvents or supplies for the lab, I was greeted with smiles, head nods, and kind words by folks who somehow looked at me as their hope, their inspiration.

Talk about having imposter syndrome...little did anyone know that I was a two-time college flunk-out!

After two-and-a-half years in the lab, I was asked to consider moving into the production operations space. It would be an opportunity to bring my technical expertise into the bulk manufacturing environment, which entailed converting from eight- to twenty-ounce containers of product to several thousand gallons of the same product.

There is plenty of room for error with mixing a small container of something – you can throw away a mistake – but an error with hundreds of gallons is both costly and dangerous.

My front office colleagues said, "Why do you want to go out there and work with all of *those* people (meaning Black folks)? You don't want to go out there. That's a dirty environment. That's a tough crowd." Several erstwhile friends – we had golfed, played basketball or bowled together – drifted away when I decided to move.

But in this new environment, I felt at home. I could apply my technical skills from the laboratory to the real world, where we could produce products to satisfy our customers' needs. I could lead people and develop teams.

Over the course of my career at Sherwin Williams, I ended up working across all three shifts.

While I had landed a good job, married Karen, and started shifting the trajectory of my life, there was still something missing.

I had walked away from the old lifestyle, but not yet experienced a complete transformation in character.

Rather than deal with life's challenges, I continued to make reckless and selfish decisions that not only hurt me but also caused considerable heartache and grief for my family.

It continued to take many years for me to realize I actually never loved myself, so how could I truly love and support others the way they needed?

To those who were there to witness and feel the pain of my transgressions, I remain deeply sorry, yet extremely grateful for their forgiveness. They helped me grow up and become the person I am today.

"Some of life's best lessons don't show up on a transcript."

College: Strike 3 or Home Run?

After nine years, my leadership at Sherwin-Williams told me that I could no longer advance without a bachelor's degree. While they had promised to pay for my degree completion, they remained unaware of my past academic struggles.

I had always found any excuse to avoid going back to school each year – getting married, buying a house, having children, etc... I wasn't even sure whether I could get admitted after that dismal University of Akron GPA. I knew that I was destined for greater things and to impact more lives, so I needed to prepare for that future.

I went back to Akron and met with the same dean who kicked me out. I told him I had grown up personally, professionally, and even more importantly, spiritually. I now had a family, a good job, and was prepared to finish what I had started so long ago.

Yet, despite all these changes, he still refused to readmit me. I returned to my car and openly wept.

I was thirty- one years old, begging God not to allow my past to define my future. In that moment, a little voice told me to go to Cleveland State University – a commuter school where the average student age was around twenty- eight years old. I hesitated.

Cleveland State, in my opinion, was just a half-step above community college! I now know that to grow in this journey called life, I needed to be humbled. Molded into a new and better version of myself.

Still weeping, I drove thirty-five minutes north on Interstate 77 from Akron to Cleveland State without an appointment. In Fenn Tower, the Office of Admissions, I approached an older woman reminiscent of my late Big Momma at the reception counter.

Without warning, I poured out my entire catalog of life's failures, lies, and infidelities in a rant of more than twenty minutes. As I look back, this was something akin to a confessional.

When I finally came up for air, I asked to schedule an appointment with the dean of admissions. I hadn't realized he was standing ten feet away and had heard everything! He motioned for me to come with him. Feeling both embarrassed and ashamed, I followed him to his office.

The course of my life was altered when he said, "I think you're exactly the type of student Cleveland State wants and needs." He invited me to apply for conditional admission, with his only request being that if accepted, I give my time, talent and treasure back to the university.

I wrote a sixteen-page essay about my life, detailing my mistakes and asking the university to give me a chance. I also submitted five letters of recommendation from friends, business colleagues, and mentors. A committee accepted me into a conditional pilot program with twenty-nine other students.

I graduated in 1996, fourteen years after my high school graduation, with a 3.97 GPA and honors.

My growing faith, my family, and my full- time job provided a focus and commitment to studying I never had at either Miami or Akron.

Since then, I have kept my promise to give back. I serve on the boards of multiple local and national non-profit community-based organizations, including the Cleveland State University Foundation Board of Trustees.

In 2020, I also established an endowed scholarship in our family's name for disadvantaged, underserved students.

Beyond academics, my CSU experience taught me a host of servant-leadership qualities, from vulnerability and authenticity to humility and transparency.

It also helped me to begin to find my purpose – to give back to my community and to share my story with young people so they don't make the same mistakes I did.

I was blessed to get three chances… Few people get more than one.

"Second chances are not always guaranteed, so make the most of each opportunity to do good for yourself and others."

Andersen Consulting/Accenture

After graduation, I was working at Sherwin-Williams when I earned a certificate in human resources from a local organization called ERC. I always knew that I would eventually work in human resources. Having been a dissatisfied customer of HR in the past, I wanted to provide my clients with a more positive and meaningful experience.

While Sherwin-Williams was considering my next-level opportunities, a recruiter for Andersen Consulting (now Accenture) contacted me about joining the company as a Senior Consultant. Andersen was trying to enhance its workforce by adding individuals with real-world industry experience to those who joined the company fresh out of college.

The role required weekly travel to clients spanning the United States and locations far outside of my comfort zone. On top of that, I had only flown three times in my entire thirty-two years of life! After consulting with my family, I decided to step out on faith and accept their offer. Luckily, my first role was within driving distance.

At my first client engagement, in a steel mill in Aliquippa, Pennsylvania, my twenty-something colleagues showed up in suits and ties while I wore steel- toed boots and a flannel shirt. I knew the factory floor.

We worked in a fully integrated steel mill that made eighteen-inch slabs and rolled them to one-sixteenth- inch coils. The environment was sometimes blazing hot, sometimes freezing cold, and always dangerous.

I gained credibility with the shop floor employees because my former coworkers at Sherwin-Williams belonged to the same steelworkers' union. In my previous role, I had sat at the bargaining table with many of their regional leaders.

Many steelworkers were in their fifties and sixties and been in the mill since high school. Some of these men and women were earning "executive level" salaries of $100-120,000 a year. Unfortunately, this very dangerous occupation led to two employee tragedies while I was there: one despondent man jumped into a vat of molten steel; the other was crushed by a coil.

It was the late 1990s. We were introducing computers to track the processing from slab to coil, replacing an antiquated system of handwritten notes taped to the material.

Men who stood six feet eight inches tall and weighed three hundred pounds were skittish about touching the keyboard and mouse.

They were used to withdrawing money from an ATM and playing games on their phones. I explained this was just another computer where they could make inputs and receive outputs. They got it. I was able to meet my clients where they were and communicate in a way that resonated with them.

It was a wonderful feeling to see the joy and sense of accomplishment on the faces of those men and women when they put aside their fears and confidently embraced this new approach to doing their jobs.

This is an example of how patience and empathy, along with non- judgmental encouragement, can drive the desired outcome.

I worked for Accenture for six years, consulting with Fortune 250 companies across the country.

I worked primarily in the areas of supply chain management and organizational change management. Much of our work involved implementing large, enterprise-wide software solutions, such as Oracle or SAP, to enable faster, smarter, more efficient business processes.

I've always excelled at building trusting relationships with customers and key stakeholders. I was able to demystify the technology and explain how it could generate a win for both employees and customers. My weekly travels with Accenture took me to many U.S. cities, large and small.

"True relationships are built not on sameness,
but on the courage to show up as you are and embrace
others for who they are."

Avon Lake

In 1998, Karen and I purchased a model home in Avon Lake, eighteen miles west of downtown Cleveland. My Mom still lived eighteen miles east of downtown Cleveland in Wickliffe. She lived alone in a house that seemed to need constant repairs. In those years, while I was commuting for Accenture, I wasn't able to visit her often enough to help maintain the house. I was able to convince her to sell the house and move into an apartment in nearby Westlake, Ohio, in 2002.

During our years in Avon Like, I continued to be active from a community perspective by coaching youth sports, including starting the little league football team that still exists to this day.

As my children got older, many of their extracurricular activities moved from being solely on weekends to taking place during the weekday afternoons and evenings.

One thing that I vividly remember was that when I was growing up, my Mom was there for everything – every sporting event, band concert, awards ceremony, etc.

The life of a consultant back in those days, and probably even to some extent now, made it difficult to always be present for your family.

I reflect in this moment while out of town for work, Karen called to tell me that our beloved dog, Teddy - a retired champion Chow, had passed away.

She had literally laid beside him on the floor, comforting him until he expired.

Two years later, shortly after my father-in-law passed away, I took a job with Limited Brands, then the parent company of The Limited, Express, Bath & Body Works, Henri Bendel, La Senza and Victoria's Secret. This role required our family to move south to Columbus, Ohio.

We invited Mom to join us on the move, but she chose to stay in Westlake.

Mom came from a generation that viewed home ownership as the ultimate fulfillment of the American Dream. She never got over the trauma of giving up her paid-for home and moving to an apartment at my insistence. I understand that now.

And, I'm sure she never forgave me...

In a very short period of time, I became personally and professionally engaged in the Columbus community.

Limited Brands recruited me to help drive the organizational change management efforts associated with an enterprise-wide transformation of new software, systems, and processes. I was already familiar with many of these software applications and systems from my experience at Accenture.

From a community perspective, I got re-engaged in coaching youth sports; my children were playing basketball and football.

The mayor later appointed me to the Community Relations Commission for the City of Columbus. It was as though I grew in stature, fame, and success immediately upon arrival.

My friend and mentor, Ellen, recently shared a quote with me that resonates now as I look back at what was going on internally during that time: "EGO = Easing God Out."

While the transition for me personally and professionally from Cleveland to Columbus was an easy one, I never quite considered what impact it might have on my wife Karen, and my children – Roslyn, Chante, and Kadell.

In very different ways, it turned out to be challenging for each of them. As parents, we often try to give our kids the things, experiences, and type of access to those things we enjoyed, as well as the things we lacked, when we were young.

We chose to reside in the northern suburbs of Columbus to be within reasonable driving distance from our parents in Greater Cleveland.

We selected a high-quality school district.

We built a home in a far more racially and ethnically diverse community than where we were coming from.

What I didn't consider were all those things that made living in Avon Lake so special for them. A unique aspect of our time in Avon Lake was that it definitely had more of a neighborhood, "everybody-knows-everybody" vibe reminiscent of my time growing up in Wickliffe.

Just as we had all been "Blue Devils," my kids had become "Shoremen and Shoregals."

At no point had I fully considered the importance of them maintaining that sense of belonging, and the very real fact that they would miss their friends, schools, teachers, coaches, and the community.

We definitely lost that sense of community when we moved to Columbus.

There are countless variables that I personally did not consider in the decision. I now realize it was largely a left-brained, analytical and process- oriented decision. I had failed to apply a whole-brain approach that would have helped me understand the spiritual, emotional, and interpersonal relationship aspects of such a move. I also realize that in those moments when I thought that I was showing up for them, I never took the time to fully listen and understand what they truly needed from me in each particular moment.

The phrase "Be Here Now" rarely applied when I engaged with them. Often, while I should have been actively listening, I would be thinking about other things, like what my next move should be or how soon I could step in to share *my* solution to their problem.

It took me a long time to realize that my children struggled with many of the same feelings of inadequacy, insecurity, and unworthiness I had experienced.

And just as I had chosen earlier to mask those things, they did the same, each in their own way.

For the sake of my loved ones, I will not describe all that happened during our time in Columbus. Thinking about where, when, and how I hurt the people I hold so dear to my heart has been painful and difficult for me to come to terms with.

It took many, many years for me to ultimately learn to forgive myself.

"The hardest lessons from our past become
the stepping stones of our future."

"Therapy can be a great thing,
so don't be afraid to ask for help."

In 2012, on a Thursday just before the winter holidays, I received a LinkedIn connection request from a guy who was the head of Talent Acquisition at Thermo Fisher Scientific.

When I looked at his profile, I noticed that he graduated from Marietta College in southern Ohio, where my eldest son was a freshman student-athlete. He was African American and had also been a student- athlete at Marietta. Since Marietta was in the southeastern tip of Ohio and the heart of Appalachia, I thought I could at least connect him with my son to develop a mentoring relationship. I accepted his invitation, and we wound up on the phone just a few hours later.

Back then, both my email address and my cellphone number were on my LinkedIn profile. It turned out we had much in common, so I was happy I had agreed to make the connection. After realizing our common points of connection, the call turned into a conversation on diversity, inclusion, and my overall philosophy regarding organizational culture.

I shared bits and pieces of having grown up in both Wickliffe and Cleveland, and how I gained a unique perspective. I explained that diversity without inclusion is meaningless, so inclusion must come first.

True inclusion requires intentionality, commitment, and effort not just from one person, but from the entire organization – board/C-suite on down.

At that time, I didn't know that Thermo Fisher was in the process of hiring its first global Chief Diversity Officer, and had already narrowed the field down to three finalists who were scheduled to be at the headquarters in Boston, Massachusetts for final interviews the following Thursday.

In just a few short hours, our conversation went from a simple "meet and greet" to an invitation to fly to Boston on Monday to meet with members of the executive leadership team, and ultimately with the CEO.

I honestly wasn't prepared for what transpired in those four days between initially meeting the recruiter and being offered a job to develop and implement a global strategy for nearly 40,000 employees across 50 countries.

I didn't even know what a good offer or reasonable counteroffer to take the job looked like. So this was definitely a leap of faith. Thermo Fisher was willing to have me work out of its Pittsburgh location, rather than move to their corporate headquarters just outside of Boston, so I could remain within driving distance of my Mom and children.

So, I accepted their offer. For the next five years, I traveled the globe with teammates, building a culture of diversity, equity, inclusion and belonging across the Thermo Fisher Scientific landscape.

In my travels, I was blessed to encounter fascinating people, places, and things.

I was also especially happy to be in a position to take my Mom across the globe with me to countries that she had only dreamed of.

I realize how fortunate I am that many of those relationships that were built during that chapter of my life are just as strong today.

"True family is built on love, not just lineage."

Cookie

After moving from Columbus to Pittsburgh to work for Thermo Fisher Scientific, I never expected to remarry, despite some of my friends' efforts to set me up – one colleague my age tried to interest me in her daughter who was eighteen years younger (I later learned such an age gap was not unusual in their culture).

On my birthday, a LinkedIn message appeared: "Happy Birthday, Alan! Don't know if you remember me…this is Valerie. You knew me as Cookie."

Did I remember her?

Valerie was my childhood sweetheart! She lived on my grandparents' street; we met when she was three and I was four. I played with her older brother. We dated for a couple of years in our late teens, but we had a nasty breakup (my fault). She never knew the hidden dark side of my life back then. I had often wondered what became of her. I happily accepted her connection request and gave her my phone number. Somehow, she lost it, so I had to resend it to her via LinkedIn.

Later, she called and we talked for over four hours, just catching up on life and reminiscing about our childhood. I felt almost like I was nineteen again.

Cookie at Age 18

Cookie had left Cleveland and moved to Chicago in the early 1990s to start a new life, with three thousand dollars in her purse and no job prospects.

She dreamed of going to the big city and carving her own path, never mind the naysayers. She eventually found success, rising through the ranks in international banking. She married a man from The Gambia, West Africa, and had a son named Evan. They later divorced, and he returned to Africa some years later without having much of a presence in his son's life.

Twelve years after she moved to Chicago, her employer decided to offshore its operations. Since her father was declining due to illness, she returned home with her son to her family in Cleveland.

To this day, Cookie never really got over leaving Chicago, where she was able to grow, thrive, and establish herself as an adult. But we agree it was divine intervention for her to return to Cleveland so we could reconnect.

When I think of what I love most about her, it is her heart. She deeply cares about all forms of life – from the fish in our two aquariums; to Jasper, our seven- year old Cavachon; to JoJo, our seventy-five-year old turtle; to the flowers, trees, and shrubs in our yard. Her strong, selfless character enabled her to take a job in Cleveland, which paid a third of her Chicago salary, take public transportation to and from work, and carry gloves and socks in her purse during the winter months to give to mothers whenever she saw their children lacking warm clothing.

After one failure at marriage, I never expected to try again. I assumed I would be alone, but not lonely. Then Cookie reentered my life. We got married on July 11, 2015. She's my rock, my biggest cheerleader, and my forever soulmate.

Our Wedding Day - July 2015

In Fall 2017, Cookie was diagnosed with an incurable illness that requires daily medication just to maintain a relatively decent quality of life.

I had just completed my MBA at the Weatherhead School of Management at Case Western Reserve University, and my global travel for Thermo Fisher Scientific had expanded to nearly forty weeks away from home. I felt my team and I had advanced the company culture to where it could sustain itself and keep growing.

I decided to take early retirement, perhaps do some teaching and public speaking, and spend time caring for my soulmate. I told the CEO what I then thought would be my last day in corporate America - May 4, 2018.

"Life will always present us with difficult decisions to be made. The key is making the ones that leave us with the fewest regrets."

MetroHealth

In late April 2018, an executive recruiter called me about an opportunity as Chief Diversity Officer at a public hospital system focused on underserved patients in the Cleveland area.

MetroHealth was the third-largest of Cleveland's Big Four health systems, which includes the second-largest VA Hospital in the United States, and the only public safety- net entity. The system received some funding from county government. Some seventy percent of patients were on Medicare or Medicaid, uninsured or woefully underinsured.

Two-thirds were black, brown, or poor and white.

I already had personal connections with MetroHealth – my mother was treated there for scarlet fever in the 1940s, my younger daughter received excellent treatment for burns after an accident, my second-oldest grandson was born there, and Evan's pediatrician worked there – she was married to a guy I grew up with in Wickliffe.

During the interview process, the CEO mentioned that he was also looking for a Chief Human Resources Officer, and that my background qualified me for both jobs.

We decided Human Resources would report to Diversity, the reverse of most organizations, and I would report directly to the CEO. The health system had fewer than seven thousand employees, compared to seventy- seven thousand at Thermo Fisher Scientific.

I completely resonated with its mission, vision, and values. Cookie urged me to accept. I joined the healthcare system in June 2018 as Senior Vice President, Chief Diversity & Human Resources Officer.

Amid the COVID-19 pandemic and the reaction to the murder of George Floyd in the Spring of 2020, we decided I should focus entirely on DEI, especially Equity, and leave human resources. I became Chief Equity Officer, later adding Community Impact to my title.

During the pandemic, disproportionate numbers of black and brown people died or went on ventilators.

Given the well-known medical atrocities that impacted communities of color over the course of U.S. history (Tuskegee syphilis experiment, Henrietta Lacks, smallpox-laced blankets, etc…), there was a high degree of resistance to getting the vaccine amid mistrust and misinformation.

Even many black and brown employees in the system were reluctant to get vaccinated. We developed an internal campaign designed specifically to address "Why am I getting vaccinated?"

For me, this was very personal. I wanted to live long enough to see my kids and grandkids grow up and lead productive lives. We aimed to engage the community, especially the churches, so that people could make more informed decisions. Our external-facing campaign to "make sure that we got the facts out about the vax" included speaking with a pastor more than ninety years old who came to the hospital for vaccination so he could live to enjoy his great-grandkids.

We even went into nursing homes, jails, homeless shelters, wherever we could engage vulnerable populations.

While we were the smallest of the large healthcare systems in our region, we vaccinated the most people – those who were also among the most vulnerable.

I remain extremely proud of how our health system responded during the Coronavirus pandemic. We saved lives.

"To whom much is given, much is required.
But even when you don't have much,
you can still make a difference."

Choosing a New Path

In summer 2016, my Case Western Reserve University EMBA cohort spent a week in Spain, then went to Greece, which was suffering a financial crisis so severe ATMs would issue no more than forty-five dollars a day. I could imagine the panic in America amid such conditions, but the Greeks were constantly partying, feasting, dancing with unabashed *joie de vivre*.

"We've been around for thousands of years," they explained. "We've weathered every storm you can imagine."

What a different worldview!

By summer 2023, I was seeking a new way forward in my own life. I was tired of the hamster-on-a-wheel corporate life; uneasy with the lack of integrity and authenticity, honesty, and ethics I saw from some leaders on a daily basis; longing for freedom, flexibility, balance, and something like the irrepressible joy I witnessed in Greece.

I embraced my role as man of the house at age three, but for my entire life, I seemed to pour out more than I received, and I felt completely depleted.

I heard an Easter sermon online during the pandemic, where the preacher recalled the airline instructions in case of emergency: "Put on your own oxygen mask before assisting others."

"If we don't take care of ourselves,
we can't be much use to the people around us."

Revelation

In September 2023, my mother was diagnosed with a very rare form of cancer.

As her only child, I knew I needed time to help get her affairs in order, develop a palliative care plan, and bring healing, peace, and closure to our often-fraught relationship.

Just a few weeks later, I was scheduled to give a keynote talk at a healthcare conference at UCLA. Cookie and I decided to add on a few vacation days after the conference to visit friends and family in Arizona. That would give me time to deal with the news of Mom's illness and my disenchantment with my professional career. I decided to take a personal retreat in the mountains above Sedona, Arizona to clear my head and seek spiritual guidance.

Sedona has always been a special place for me, where I feel the splendor of God's presence in red desert mountains and foothills.

Sedona, Arizona

Before we left, I envisioned some kind of cinematic "burning bush" experience where God would show me exactly what direction to take, the *Ten Commandments* movie scene where Charlton Heston comes down the mountain with a full head of silver hair looking transfigured. I would speak in Los Angeles on Wednesday, hang out with Cookie's cousins in Goodyear on Thursday, drive up to Sedona with our childhood friend on Friday, and chill in Scottsdale on Saturday.

On Thursday morning, our plans changed. Cookie's cousins, who moved to Arizona a few years earlier, had never visited Sedona. They wanted to make the trip, over two hours, with us a day earlier, and we agreed. I needed to make my mountaintop pilgrimage during the day to avoid rattlesnakes, scorpions, coyotes, mountain lions, and other dangers – this was not a shopping or sightseeing excursion for me – but we got a late start from Goodyear and faced traffic congestion, construction, and delays. It took more than three hours to reach Sedona, despite my pushing the speed limit whenever possible. I wanted to drop off Cookie and her cousins and rush to the mountain before the sun set, but one cousin asked for a bathroom break just as we entered Sedona. So, I turned into a Speedway gas station for a quick break and a bottle of water.

Now this was no ordinary gas station/convenience store – there was a high-end jewelry store inside with diamonds, silver, gold, and even top of the line watches! Nevertheless, my mission was to go to the bathroom, buy a bottle of water, and move on.

While I waited for the others, I browsed the twenty-foot jewelry counter and noticed framed faith-based quotes and Bible texts on the walls, as well as a section to the right with a wide variety of faith-based jewelry, such as crosses and stars of David.

I approached one of the two women behind the counter and asked, "Who came up with the idea of putting a high- end jewelry store inside a gas station?" She explained that she and her husband, co-owners of the store, decided years earlier to close their shop in New York City and retire to Arizona, but they started over from scratch with the opportunity to re-imagine their business. They were friends with the gas station owner, who gave them the space. As we chatted, I noticed a white gold his-and-hers bracelet set depicting the Ten Commandments with Roman numerals on each link, and thought it would be a cool stocking stuffer, Christmas gift for me and my wife.

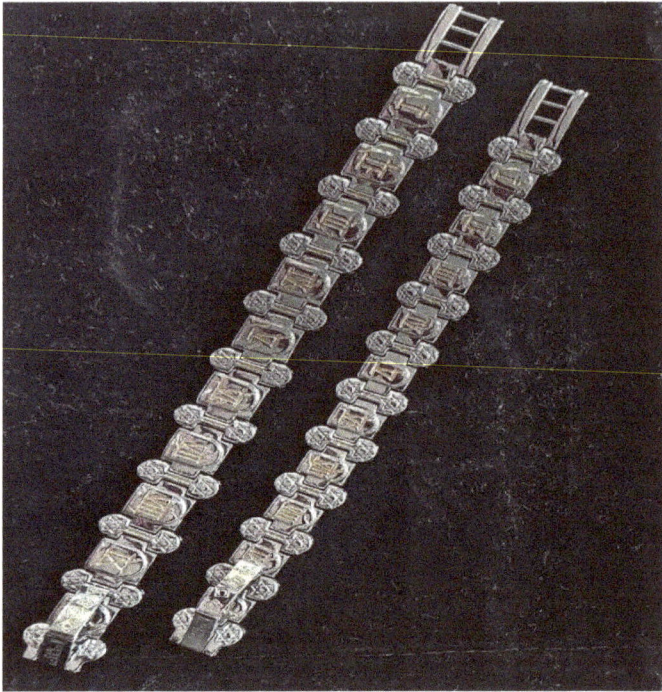

The Bracelets

When Cookie and her cousins joined us at the counter, Cookie struck up a conversation with the other woman, who immediately told her: "I sensed your spirit the moment you walked into this gas station." Cookie told her why we were in Sedona and why I was eager for a personal and professional retreat.

She introduced me to the woman, Lora, and I felt an almost angelic sense of warmth and compassion from her, reminiscent of my encounter years earlier with the older woman in the Office of Admissions at Cleveland State University. I shared my whole life story, nearly sixty years in the making, to explain why this retreat was so vital.

Then Lora told me her story. She was a friend of the store owner and stopped by a few days a week to help out if needed. She and her husband, Dick, had moved in retirement to Sedona, where they owned a very large house and a much smaller one. He had felt called to ministry at age seventy-one, and they had turned the larger home into a place for open worship and Bible study. Now they were selling it. We talked for more than three hours, while Cookie and her cousins talked to the store owner, with no sense of time passing – no customers, no calls, no texts.

Time had literally stood still! The aperture of my lens was focused on Lora's face and nothing else. I didn't even realize that the sun had already set until Lora asked about our plans for the next day.

In that moment, I realized the spiritual revelation I had sought was happening in this gas station, not on a mountaintop.

Cookie and I made arrangements to have lunch with Lora and Dick the next day on Friday. "I know he will have a word for you," she told me.

The next morning, Lora called from Sedona and said we should meet them at the Pappadeaux's Seafood Kitchen in Phoenix at 11 a.m.

To my surprise, Cookie said, "I'm not supposed to go with you to that meeting. I don't want to potentially be a distraction, because whatever message God has is for YOU, and you alone. My job is to support you in whatever it is that he has planned for you."

"Are you sure?", I asked. "Yes.", she said.

They were on their way south from Sedona, a little over two hours away. I set out on the seventeen-minute drive to the restaurant. We arrived simultaneously at 10:53 a.m. and parked next to each other without prior knowledge of each other's vehicles.

From the moment I met Dick, I knew I had to let go and let God. He kept saying, "When God tells you to move, you don't hesitate, you don't question, you just trust, believe, and go." He told me about his twenty-year military career, retiring as a Major General, about his corporate success as a senior executive in the automotive industry, about his constant commitment to community and serving the underserved. He was nineteen years older than I, but we shared much in common in terms of personal mission, vision, and values.

Then he explained they were selling the big house because God had told them to move to Little Rock, Arkansas, where they had never lived, and launch a leadership development academy focused on integrity and ethics.

As he described his frustration with corporate types and academicians who sacrificed their values, beliefs, dignity, and self-respect to "win" in their field, it resonated with my own corporate experience and the testimony to young people that I have often shared as a public speaker across the country.

Where we had lunch at Pappadeaux Seafood Kitchen

I knew God wanted me to support Dick and Lora's initiative.

Lora said, "Last night when I got home, I told my husband about you and we began to pray. We prayed until about 1:30 a.m. and then fell asleep. I woke up out of a deep sleep at 3:30 a.m. and was immediately drawn to a particular piece of scripture, in a particular version of the Bible that I'd like for you to read aloud."

It was Psalms 37, a total of forty verses, in *The Passion Translation of the Bible*. As I read, I felt God was reiterating everything I had been feeling and experiencing for years, on top of my struggles with my Mom's terminal diagnosis.

When I finished, Dick said, "You know you have to quit your job when you get back home." In that moment, I felt a huge weight fall from my shoulders, and my ongoing tension vanished.

This was indeed "the peace that surpasses all understanding" that scripture talks about.

"Okay," I said.

We went home on Sunday, I submitted my resignation on Monday, and I left the company thirty days later.

"When we look close enough, we will see God's hand at work in every situation of our lives."

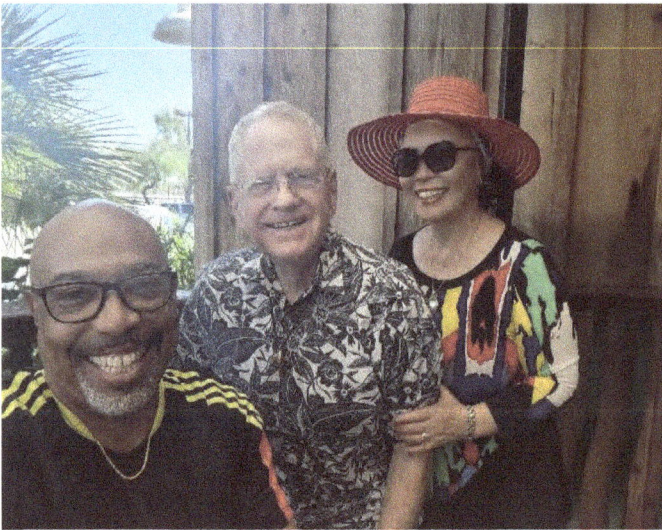

With Dick and Lora Snider

Final Chapter Before A New Beginning

On November 11, 2023, I moved from a high-paying good job to unemployment, while trying to care for my Mom and make ends meet. There was no parachute; I walked away with only five-and-a-half weeks of accrued vacation pay. This was indeed an exercise in faith.

I remember the late Dr. Charles Stanley's levels of faith: Little Faith, Great Faith, and Perfect Faith. Little Faith is when you know God can do something, but you're not sure he will. Great Faith is when you know he can and he will, but maybe he needs your "help" along the way. Perfect Faith says, "It's already taken care of!"

Dick reminded me that God loved me and had taken care of me not only in my high points, but especially during the lows. Why would he abandon me now for doing what I knew was right?

My last six months with my Mom were a journey of resilience. She was always my "Shero," but our relationship had its contentious moments.

Mom couldn't overcome many of the demons in her life and often took out her frustrations on those who loved her most. This had been true across my life, but it still hurt. She was angry with everyone and everything, from the doctors and nurses who cared for her to my family and me. She was angry about the hard life that left dreams unfulfilled – caring for siblings at a young age, giving up a dance career in New York City, divorcing my father, watching my academic failures, and more.

I was determined to ensure dignity and respect for Mom's transition, and I would smooth out the path the best way I could to honor her. I had to depend on God to carry me through those times when I wanted to give up.

On May 22, 2024, I left home at 5:45 a.m. and drove two hours to give the keynote speech for a multicultural mental health advocacy conference. The night before, we moved Mom back to hospice because the end was near. I told her I prayed for her to set aside the anger that had consumed her for years and to find peace with God.

That ended up being our last conversation, as the nurses gave her a large dose of morphine, and she went to sleep.

I was giving my speech when Mom transitioned peacefully to be with the Lord, one month and one day shy of her ninetieth birthday.

On June 22nd, we held a birthday party and celebration of her life:

- During her adolescent and teen years, she studied interpretive modern dance at Karamu House, the oldest active African American theater and performing arts venue in the United States.

- She graduated from John Adams High School in Cleveland, Ohio, in 1953, and furthered her academic education at Central State University and Lake Erie College, earning a Bachelor of Science degree in Chemistry.

- She made history as the first Black, first female Analytical Research Chemist for the Lubrizol Corporation, where she dedicated twenty-eight years of her career.

- She was deeply involved in her community, serving as a deacon and fourth-grade Sunday school teacher at Wickliffe Presbyterian Church.

- She volunteered extensively and served on several boards, including the Wickliffe Outlook Club, NOACA (Northern Ohio Area-Wide Coordinating Agency), Lake County Branch of the NAACP, City of Wickliffe Parks and Recreation Committee, and the Cleveland Section of the American Chemical Society, where she held the positions of Vice Chair and Secretary.

- She was a passionate lover of jazz, cooking, and the fine arts.

Dancing at Karamu House

Dancing at Karamu House

The day of the party started rough, an exercise in resilience for me. The venue was not adequately staffed. The air conditioning failed on a humid day, with temperatures above ninety degrees.

Just before the event, I discovered someone had stolen four hundred dollars I had left on my porch to pay a friend for services. Then my brother-in-law rushed in to say my daughter and grandson had been in a highway accident with a semi truck. I hurried to the scene and thankfully found them uninjured.

Through it all, I kept my focus on celebrating Mom.

As my dear mentors, Audra and Donna, had taught me:

"It's not about the stimulus; it's the response."

Evelyn Juanita Nevel

June 23, 1934 – May 22, 2024

INTETHIQ

In November 2023, I founded INTETHIQ (pronounced in/teh/thick), whose name unites integrity, ethics, equity, and authenticity. It is a company that intentionally upholds the values of diversity, equity, inclusion, and belonging for ALL.

INTETHIQ aims to work with leaders in healthcare, manufacturing, consumer packaged goods, and academia, as well as corporate and nonprofit boards. The goal is to renew and strengthen the personal and social qualities necessary for thriving organizations and communities. Our work includes delivering keynote talks on topics such as culture, leadership, and talent; HR and Diversity, Equity and Inclusion assistance from strategy development through implementation and measurement; and leadership development and executive coaching.

I have also become an adjunct professor at Case Western Reserve University, teaching an online healthcare MBA course entitled "Introduction to Population Health".

These are all opportunities to share the culmination of what I have learned over the years. In 2009, I studied at the African American Leadership Academy in Columbus, where I learned, among other things, that mantra at the heart of resilience:

"It's not the stimulus, it's the response."

People and circumstances don't make you angry.

Your anger is how you choose to respond to people and circumstances.

They don't drive you to drink. Your drinking is your reaction to them – and it delays the necessary change.

I learned from John M., my beloved "Pops", mentor, friend and fraternity brother, what would become my daily personal affirmation:

"I deliver infinite value every day in everything and in every way.

I deliver value in how I live my life.

I deliver value in how I express my love for others.

I deliver value to my family, to my friends, to my fraternity, to my job, and to my community.

Why?

Because I am infinitely valuable!"

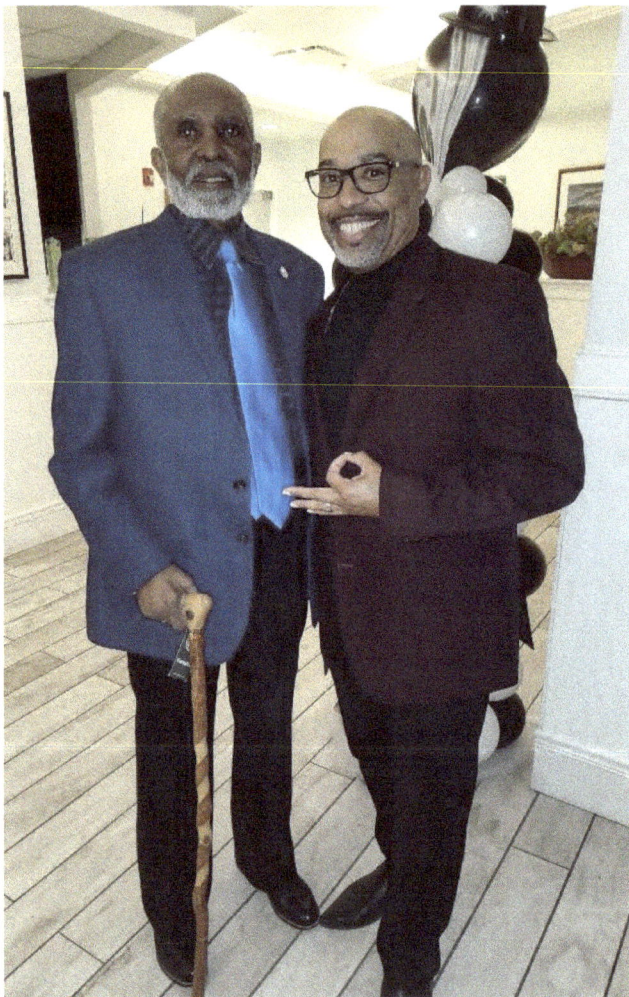

With John M - aka "OG", aka "Pops"

Those are more than words. They are who I am inside. If I find myself no longer delivering value in my environment, it's time to move on. It's not about running away from something or someone. It's about giving yourself permission to go to a place where you truly belong.

INTETHIQ is a calling, not just a paycheck. I chose a life change, not a job change. I want to use my God- given gifts and experiences in the most effective, comprehensive way I can, far more fully than the typical corporate structure.

Tomorrow is not promised to any one of us, so what you do today is what truly matters.

What you do, as well as how you choose to do it, defines your legacy, hence my personal motto:

"Aspire to inspire before you expire,
because if not now – when?"

Resonant Leadership

Since the age of three, I have been learning about leadership. The old top-down, threatening, my-way-or-the-highway style – elements of dissonant leadership – is rightly fading away as empowered workers demand a more humane workplace. I remember trying to mediate between such oppressive kingdom-builders and their employees sometimes in my human resources work, especially when it was not united with Diversity, Equity and Inclusion work.

I had a boss like that at the paint and coatings company. He would sneak into the shop around two or three in the morning and hide in an empty fifty-five-gallon drum behind the fill room to spy on whether workers were napping or wasting time. I saw him peeping out from under the lid when I worked the late shift. In a way, it was a laughable waste of his time and energy. But to me, that meant he didn't trust us – and the feeling became mutual.

When we sent many hospital employees to work from home during COVID-19, different trust levels among management became clear.

Some leaders came from companies that had employees that often worked-from-home and considered it to be no big deal. Others assumed the employees would cheat us: "How do we know they're not going to be watching TV all day?" It turned out that some people were even more productive – they might take breaks during the day, but they were checking emails at night and improving efficiency.

Great leaders are those you can trust. We had a doctor at MetroHealth who had great influence on employees because they knew they could trust them. That's an element of resonant leadership. And it's why I focus on being my true authentic self with everyone, regardless of whether they come to like me or not.

A resonant leader inspires you to play above your skill level.

No matter how far they have gone in their career, they are still humble, still open to learn, and still eager to grow.

When they need to correct someone's behavior, they treat the person like an equal adult, not like a child. When the mistake is corrected, they move on. They're so determined to be authentic that they're willing to be vulnerable, to admit when they're wrong, to acknowledge what they don't know, to seek the wisdom of others.

Their goal is not conquest, but the common good. A leader who cares about their organization doesn't punch the clock after eight hours every day. You continue caring about the people, keeping up with what's going on. You're driven by mission and purpose, not just a paycheck. I think a leader with these qualities can succeed in any industry.

Any leader in an organization must ensure their employees are safe, heard, understood, and supported whenever they need the leader to remove the roadblocks to their job success.

Those four things are a hierarchy of needs in the workplace. To provide them, the leader must guard their safety, listen to their needs, respond in a way that upholds their dignity, and affirm their value to the organization.

That means, for example, supplying the tools they need to do their job well, without balking at the cost. The leader must keep track of their own self- awareness and their personal barriers to treating the employees well, including the mistreatment the leader might have suffered in their own life or work. They need to break the cycle, not perpetuate it.

They were not chosen for leadership, just so they could inflict emotional pain and suffering on others.

Employees' safety must not depend on their submissiveness, as if they were children who should be seen and not heard. Most of us spend more time at work versus being able to spend it with our friends, family and loved ones.

So, work should not be merely a place to keep your head down, stay out of trouble, and earn a paycheck.

Sometimes, for the good of the person as well as the good of the organization, you have to let someone go.

Even then, you can treat them with dignity and respect their humanity.

An old story about Cleveland Browns co-founder and first coach Paul Brown tells of a time in the 1940s when the team bus driver got hopelessly lost, leaving the team running late for the stadium. "I'm sorry, Coach," the driver told Brown, who was standing at the front of the bus. "I know you're mad at me." "I'm not mad at you," Brown said. "I'm mad at the person who hired you."

Across my career, I have worked for leaders I deeply admire and some leaders for whom I have zero respect.

I have assembled my own leadership style from elements of the best. I know how to be collaborative and consensus-seeking, and I know how to make the tough calls while upholding the dignity and respect of every person.

I have mentored hundreds of people in my career, some ongoing since the early 1990s.

The longstanding ones might connect only a couple of times a year; the newer ones start on a schedule.

People seem to find me easy to talk with, and I'm happy to help as much as I can. I've mentored literally hundreds of people in the companies that I have worked for. We usually talk about careers, personal life, professional issues and strategies.

I also encourage people to find sponsors who can advocate on their behalf to successfully move up in their company. This has been very gratifying, as some have gone on to achieve much higher positions than mine.

These are always mutually beneficial relationships, not one-way. A good mentor recognizes how much they can learn from listening to their mentee's perspectives.

"Mentoring is a two-way street where wisdom flows in both directions. The mentor shares experiences, the mentee brings fresh perspectives, and together, they create a cycle of growth and learning that benefits both."

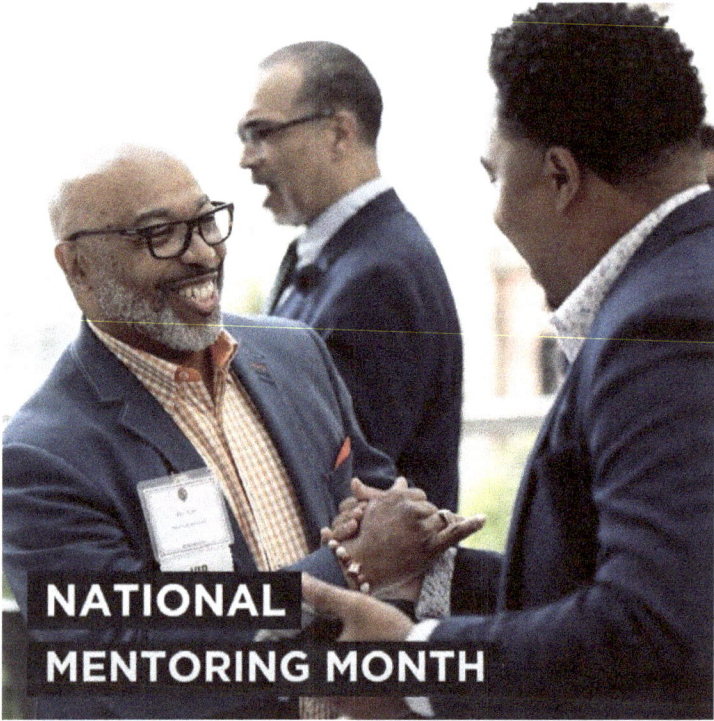

NATIONAL
MENTORING MONTH

A Life of Continuous Learning

Like many of my peers, I have a personal board of directors. These are the people who keep it real with me, regardless. They are John M., Jerry X, Ms. Audra, Vince, KC, Donnie B., Ellen, KMF, Donna and Todd.

I can go to them when I'm discouraged, restless, or in need of a kick in the behind to keep moving forward. These relationships are much easier for me now because I don't mind allowing them to see me being vulnerable.

I'm more likely to share particular things with certain ones, based on our shared lived experiences. This means I intentionally tap into my network of people who have gone through similar challenges to learn from their experience.

For a big thing like a career move, I'll talk to them all. I think it's important, on both sides, to have a clear point of view. While the other person might not always agree with your perspective, they should certainly respect and appreciate your input.

Vulnerability matters when you're serving as the mentor, too. One of my mentees was going through a divorce and wondering how to relate to his twin sons. I talked to him about my experience of being kept away from my dad as a child and encouraged him to find ways to sustain the connection.

People need to know that your life is not perfect, no matter their perception of your achievements.

I believe we also need someone to be our therapist, professional or not – a person who can look at things objectively and listen to us without judgment.

That probably means not a friend or family member. My therapist, for example, helped me avoid getting triggered when my Mom threw up my failed college experiences or urged me, even in my late fifties, to take the MCATs and become a pediatrician. My reaction to that is my responsibility. Talking it out with someone who doesn't have a personal stake in the game always helps.

Over the years, I have developed a step-by-step strategy for the first eighteen to twenty-four months in a new role or new organization.

The first three months is about getting to understand your responsibilities, objectives, benchmarks, team purpose, performance metrics, and other basics to align your approach with expectations.

Develop a proactive relationship with your human resources representative.

Break down your goals to thirty-, sixty-, ninety-day increments. If you want to establish regular touch-bases with your boss, schedule them yourself, rather than waiting for someone else to take the initiative.

Next, plan out the next three to six months.

By now, you should know who are the highest performers and who are the strongest influencers – knowing that these are not necessarily the same people.

Identify your next-stage move and create an individual development plan to achieve it.

Figure out how to capture and document feedback. Then consider the next six to twelve months, when you will be getting your mid-year review, and then twelve to eighteen months, when you'll have your annual review and receive new goals.

I have several additional home-grown, professional development tools that I've used to help not only myself, but countless mentees over the years.

Those will be in my next book.

> *"Lifelong learning is the key to growth – each day is an opportunity to improve, evolve, and become a better version of ourselves. The journey never ends, and neither should our desire to learn."*

Our Shared Humanity

In today's world of tweets, retweets, and endless soundbytes, the words Diversity, Equity, and Inclusion now have a negative connotation and often draw a downright visceral response.

My approach to Diversity, Equity and Inclusion is rooted in our shared human experience on this planet that, for me, goes all the way back to growing up with my friends in Wickliffe who didn't look like me.

All of us have experienced exclusion in some form, maybe being picked last for a kickball team because you were skinny or chubby or wore thick glasses. That's how exclusion because of color, gender, sexuality, or nationality feels – isolating, humiliating, demeaning – so everyone should be able to find an empathetic human connection with others. Feeling a sense of inclusion and belonging is for everybody, white men as well as minorities.

It requires us to listen to one another not only with the head, but also with the heart.

We have many ways to talk about diversity, many strategies for inclusion, and an ever-growing set of initials to describe our work (DEI, DEIJ, DEIB), but what we're really talking about is ensuring that everyone is able to live their best life, both at home and at work, and ultimately have an opportunity to realize their full potential.

It is not a separate focus, but integral to everything we do. An older friend, a widower, once told me, "I know I will die alone, but I don't want to die lonely."

I believe every person, introverts as well as extroverts, seeks human connection.

We all want to belong.

When we rule out some people because they appear to be different from us, we are limiting our own chances for connection. Happiness comes from celebrating our shared humanity.

Most of the differences are not natural, but constructed, for good or ill, and none of them are more important than our common good and solidarity.

Nothing is wrong with belonging to a group, but plenty is wrong with labeling one an in-group and the other an out-group.

Whatever our past, we can choose to be good people. As a person with my own checkered past, I am open to hiring others who have made serious mistakes, even those who may have had run-ins with the criminal justice system.

Remember that every person who is locked up and behind bars isn't necessarily guilty of having committed some heinous act. All too often, we are seeing people exonerated for crimes they didn't commit, long after they have spent the majority of their adult years hoping someone would believe in them. In some situations, the wrongfully convicted but now released person receives a token amount of compensation.

No matter how much, that money doesn't make up for all of the time that they lost. That lost time has a downstream impact not only on that person, but also on their family. Eventually, every person on this planet will make bad decisions. Some people get exposed; some won't.

Not getting caught doesn't necessarily make you a better person than those who get caught.

To bring your whole self to work requires confidence that the culture provides a level of physical and psychological safety, so you don't have to hide who you are – going back to those black and brown folks who tried to "pass" for white in order to get by and be treated fairly, to those who may self-identify as queer, to those who have relatives in poverty, prison, or any other difference.

You shouldn't have to code switch your self-understanding or behavior to be your authentic self when you leave work. You are enough and you matter.

Diversity, Equity and Inclusion work should not be difficult. No one honestly doubts the racial divisions in our nation. So let's just be honest with one another for a moment - Try to imagine if people of color had attacked the Capitol on January 6, 2021 – there is absolutely no chance they could have scaled the walls and made it inside. For many people with privilege, simply hearing the word "equity" feels like it's some kind of oppression.

Some likely fear that minorities will turn the tables and treat them like they have treated minorities once our demographic direction makes this a majority-minority nation. But the goal is to end oppression, not become oppressors. Equity is not about revenge.

It is not about having one person "lose" in order for the other to "win." Sure, there will be some loud, angry voices for score-settling, but my faith tells me they will not prevail. Look at the example of Dr. Martin Luther King Jr.

Living in a divided society is not good for the majority anymore than for minority groups.

We can tear down the walls without tearing up the fabric of our community. I believe with all my heart that love, compassion, empathy, and a universal, non-partisan, human-centered commitment to fairness can unite our diverse nation at this crucial time.

Every day, we see or hear people trying to convince one another that your perspectives or beliefs are either black or white, right or wrong.

And if you happen to disagree with their point of view, you *must* be a terrible person.

Rather than dialogue, discord results. When engaging with someone who may have a difference of opinion, I believe we have an opportunity to seek to understand not only what they feel, but also why they feel that way.

The goal should not necessarily be to change the other person's mind, thereby creating a win-lose scenario, but to enlarge and unpack the two different perspectives.

This requires empathetic listening, allowing oneself to be vulnerable and offering an ounce of grace.

For example, someone might ask, "What's wrong with saying Blue Lives Matter?" Maybe that person comes from a long line of high-integrity police officers. Because Blue Lives Matter is usually a retort to Black Lives Matter, it's important to understand WHY Black Lives Matter.

Maybe your dialogue partner agrees, or comes to agree, that Black Lives Matter is a proper focus in the context of Black people dying violently, sometimes at the hands of police.

Maybe you can agree that Blue Lives Matter is a proper focus in the context of upright police who serve and protect their community.

Even if you don't agree, you can both gain a better understanding of what the other person means and part with mutual respect for their humanity. You do not have to endorse the slogan if its intent is to hurt or offend. Issues of human equality and dignity are not really open to "agree to disagree."

My faith gives me a model of hope for the future. It teaches me to forgive, to offer grace and mercy, and to see the image of God in every person. I do not believe in dividing humanity by religions, cultures, ethnicities, beliefs or denominations. The God I worship accepts and loves us all equally.

"Faith keeps us grounded, hope keeps us moving forward, and grace allows us to walk together with understanding. When we give each other grace, we create space for growth, healing and deeper connection."

The Soundtrack of My Life

My life has had many soundtracks, beginning with my Mom's diverse musical tastes ranging from jazz, blues, and soul, to classical and rock.

Since I was about three, I remember listening to everything from Miles, Bird, Coltrane, Dizzy, Jimmy Smith, Lee Morgan and The Three Sounds to Rachmaninoff, Tchaikovsky, Bach, Beethoven, Handel, and Mozart. And Saturday morning chores were accompanied by a compilation of Blue Note records. I still have many of those vinyl albums to this day.

My childhood soundtrack also included R&B and Rock and Roll, from James Brown, Aretha, Jackson Five, Sly & The Family Stone, Isaac Hayes, Marvin Gaye, Isley Brothers, Al Green, Fifth Dimension, War, Chaka Khan & Rufus, George Clinton, Parliament-Funkadelic, P-Funk All Stars, and Commodores, to Beatles, Grand Funk Railroad, Carlos Santana, Doobie Brothers, Rolling Stones, Chicago, Rolling Stones, Kiss, AC/DC, Zeppelin, Bowie, Genesis, and of course Prince.

From those early beginnings, my musical interests continued to broaden with the birth of hip-hop and smooth jazz. From Kurtis Blow, Run DMC, Big Daddy Kane, The Beastie Boys, Biz Markie, MC Lyte, LL Cool J, Eric B & Rakim, EPMD, A Tribe Called Quest, WuTang Clan, to Biggie and 2Pac. From David Sanborn, Bob James, Earl Klugh, Ramsey Lewis, Return to Forever and Chuck Mangione to Boney James, Brian Culbertson, Rick Braun, Bob Baldwin, Norman Brown, Steve Cole and Gerald Albright. All of these artists contributed to my appreciation for diversity and my overall world view.

Putting this soundtrack in the context of amazing experiences that I've had meeting and working with people from literally all over the globe, I believe that it has given me the opportunity to better understand that our shared humanity is indeed our common ground.

To me, music is like the basic stitch in sewing, which holds two pieces of fabric together.

My love and appreciation for music led me to begin playing alto, tenor, and soprano saxophone at age eleven, having played in bands comprised of diverse people and musical genres.

One of these days, I plan to go back to basics and start taking individual private lessons again, because for me, music takes me to my happy place.

It is indeed a place of refuge for me.

My Alto Saxophone (Made in 1915)

Epilogue

My life story is not yet complete.

The story of INTETHIQ is just beginning.

There is so much more to be told. I spent much of my life either trying to self- destruct or chase the American Dream, and I paid the price.

It looks like success from the outside: I've owned expensive vehicles, built houses, traveled the world, made more money than most, but at what cost?

And who were the people that left an indelible impression on me even when I least appreciated it?

Mr. and Mrs. Clemons? JuJu and Mr. John?
Mrs. Feltham? Mr. Gilmore? Mr. Bishop? Dusty?
Dr. Jindal?

And why did they often see more in me than I saw in myself?

And most importantly, how does my relationship and trust in the Lord continue to grow and manifest itself through my daily interactions with my fellow human beings?

These stories and more, I'll share later. Until then, I pray this story has benefited you and how you approach whatever number of hours, days, months, or years you have left on this planet.

Every one of us can *DO* better.

Every one of us can *BE* better.

Each new day is our opportunity *FOR* better.

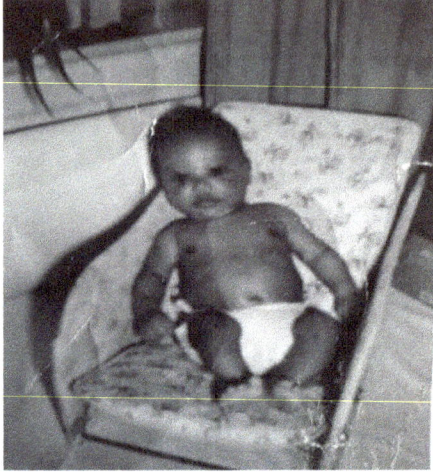

Baby Alan

Toddler Alan

Age 4

Wrestling at Age 10

High School Graduation – 1982

Case Western Reserve University MBA - 2017 w/ Carol

Dinner with Mom in Tokyo, Japan (2013)

Hanging out in Shanghai, China (2014)

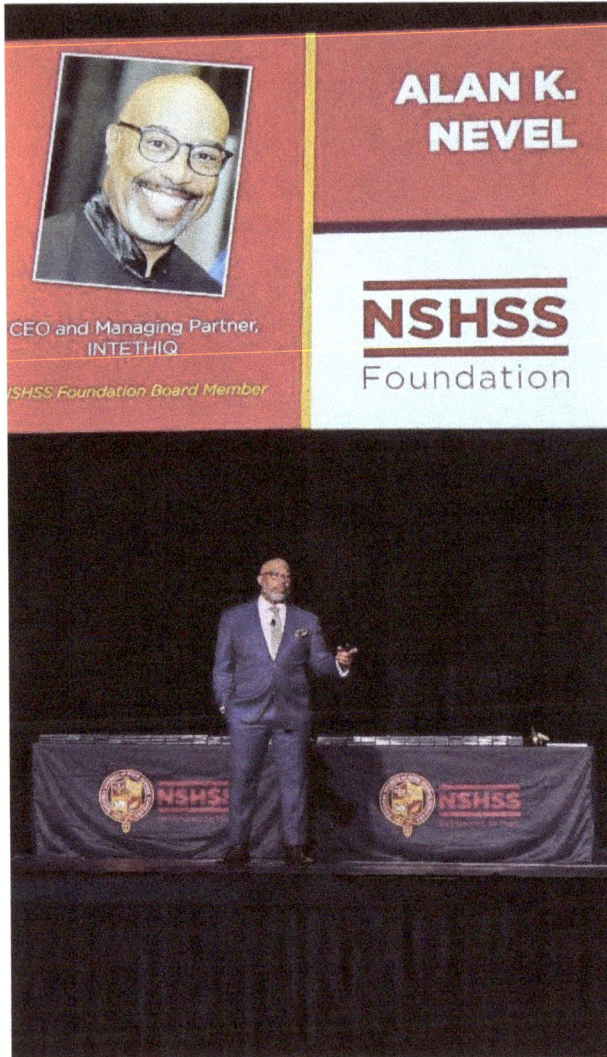

Speaking at NSHSS
Scholars Day Event in Washington DC – 2024

TV News Interview at MetroHealth – 2019

Public Speaking – 2022

TV News Interview – 2023

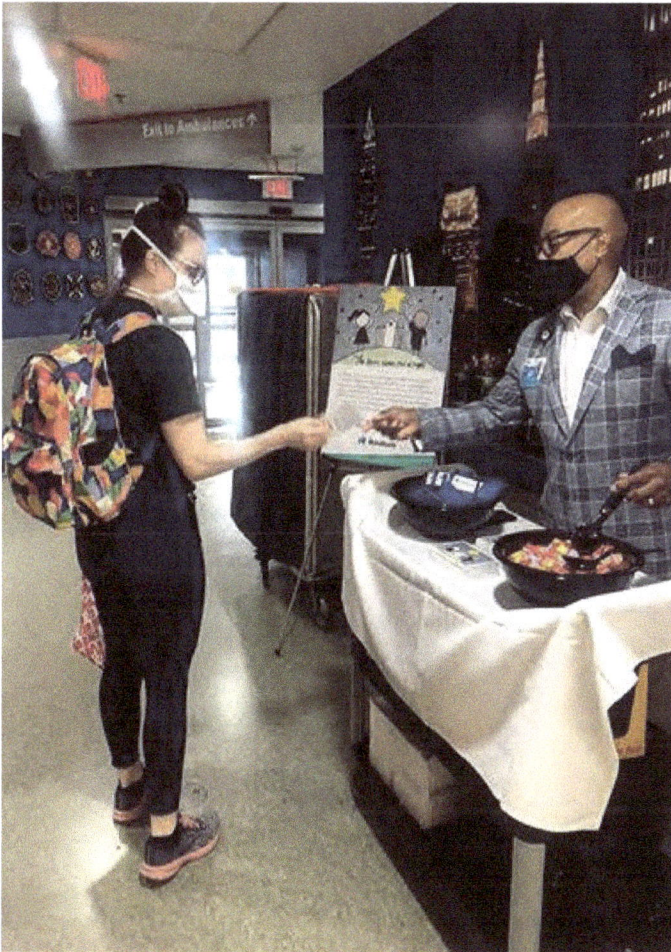

Supporting Our First Responders - 2021

LIVING MY TRUTH